THE SHAW SAVILL

Images in Mast, Steam and Motor

RICHARD P. DE KERBRECH

SHIP PICTORIAL PUBLICATIONS
1992

Cover: The DOMINION MONARCH leaving Wellington for the last time in March 1962, with paying -off pennant flying. (Shaw Savill Society)

DEDICATION: To Richard

First Published in 1992 by Ship Pictorial Publications
3 College Close, Coltishall, Norfolk NR12 7DT

© Copyright R. P. de Kerbrech 1992

British Library Cataloguing in Publication Data
de Kerbrech, R. P.
   The Shaw Savill Line: Images in Mast, Steam and Motor

        ISBN 0 9516038 3 3

Ship Pictorial Series
S.P.P.1   The Cunard Line (Peter W. Woolley & Terry Moore)
S.P.P.2   The Union-Castle Line (Alan S. Mallett)
S.P.P.3   The White Star Line (Paul Louden-Brown)
S.P.P.4   The Shaw Savill Line (Richard de Kerbrech)

Typesetting by Rosemary Klein

Printed by Page Bros, Norwich

INTRODUCTION

It is hoped that "Images in Mast, Steam and Motor" is not too grand a sub-title for what is essentially a picture book. Unfortunately for some, there are too few pictures of sailing vessels. Perhaps their appearance evokes thoughts of the "romance" of sail although whatever was romantic about the harsh conditions of windjammer mariners, one will never know.

The loss of fingernails during the shortening of canvas; manning the yards in mountainous seas and ice cold winds whilst rounding Cape Horn, together with the lack of fresh fruit and meat, must have attracted a certain breed of person.

Then there were the coal burners with their tall natural draught funnels and open promenade decks with vertical stanchions. One can only imagine the filth and coal dust everywhere during the "coaling" of the ship. Also during an era before air-conditioning life in the crew's and Passengers' quarters and engine room must have been unbearable especially when steaming down the Red Sea or in the Tropics.

Later came the innovative motorships with the all pervading smell of diesel oil throughout the lower accommodation and the inescapable oil stained boiler suits of the engine room staff. Following the Second World War the classic British passenger-cargo vessel design continued, typified by the lack of streamlining, even up until the late 1950s. The selection of pictures ends with the OCEAN MONARCH, as beyond this point Shaw Savill ceased passenger carrying activities.

This publication is not a definitive Company history of Shaw Savill & Albion, nor is it a complete fleet list but simply a selection of pictorial images of the "old" Shaw Savill Line; more of a tribute to a Company with a history that has now passed into history.

They've all gone now, those vessels with their vestigial White Star livery, so well known in London Docks, Southampton and in Australian and New Zealand waters up to the mid-1970s. Perhaps this modest little publication will make a suitable epitaph.

Richard de Kerbrech
Hill Head, Hampshire
August 1992

The **DOMINION MONARCH** outward bound off Greenhithe passing the **CUTTY SARK** and training ship H.M.S. WORCESTER (A.S. Mallett & A.C.Reed collections)

A SHORT HISTORY OF THE SHAW SAVILL LINE

Nearly twenty years after the establishment of New Zealand as a separate colony in 1841, vessels chartered by Shaw Savill & Company were carrying passengers and cargo to the Antipodes.

Early in 1858 Mr. Robert Ewart Shaw and Mr. Walter Savill resigned from the ship-broking firm of Willis, Gann and Company and set up in business for themselves as Shaw Savill & Company with modest offices at 24, Billiter Street, London.

Their knowledge of the New Zealand trade was extensive and they therefore specialised in and confined their activities to New Zealand sailings, with great success. Although primarily cargo brokers, the Partners always watched the opportunities of the passenger trade. As early as 1859 several of the cargo ships they loaded or chartered carried emigrants and for this part of the business they took the name of "The Passengers' Line of Packets".

One of the features of the New Zealand Government's settlement policy from its earliest days was the careful selection and strict regulation of its immigrants. Shaw Savill & Co., with the idea of a regular service constantly in mind, always obtained the best available ships for the purpose and paid strict attention to the selection and welfare of the emigrants travelling by their ships.

Although in those early days the Line possessed no ships of its own, it adopted as its House flag the first ensign chosen by Maori chiefs in 1834 as the National flag for the colony and replaced by the Union flag in 1840. This flag was worn by all Shaw Savill vessels.

The discovery of gold in New Zealand in the late 1850s and early 1860s led to a rush of emigrants but the strict New Zealand regulations rendered impossible the undesirable features of the earlier gold rushes to California and Australia. In 1862 Shaw Savill despatched no fewer than 45 sailing ships to New Zealand, varying in size from the 285 tons of the PLANTER to the 1,320 tons of the MERMAID, with passage times from 87 days by the CHILE to 175 days by the MESSINA. The comfort and fares in this very miscellaneous fleet naturally varied greatly and ranged from 75 guineas for a First-class single-berth cabin and from £25 Second class. In the Steerage it was £20 for a berth in an enclosed cabin and £16 a head in open berths.

In the following year they despatched no less than 69 sailing ships, the average size being considerably larger than in 1862. During this year they secured the Government contract to carry emigrants to Otago. The fare was £13.10s. from London although it was only £12 from Glasgow in spite of the railway fare, on account of the rivalry of the Albion Line vessels which sailed from there.

During the Maori Wars of 1860-1864 its vessels took British troops and war material to New Zealand.

Of the many ships chartered in 1873 by Shaw Savill & Company the most noteworthy was the iron-screw steamer MONGOL, a new ship of 2,260 tons gross which made the passage from London to Otago in 58 days. This was the first real commercial voyage by a full-powered steamer on the New Zealand service.

The competition between Shaw Savill and Patrick Henderson's Albion Line of Glasgow which had been trading as early as 1855 kept high the standard of efficiency and comfort of passengers and the prices low, between them they enjoyed almost a monopoly of the New Zealand trade. This was disliked by a number of colonial merchants and in 1873 they formed the New Zealand Shipping Company (N.Z.S.Co.). This new competition, rendered more dangerous by local patriotism, was met by the two British companies by the chartering, buying and building of vessels.

The offer by the New Zealand Government of a subsidy for direct steam communication between England and that country and the growing competition of the New Zealand Shipping Company brought about the amalgamation of the two British Lines, and in November 1882 the Shaw Savill & Albion Company Ltd., was formed.

The main purpose of the new Company was to build and run steamers but the 31 sailing ships taken over from the two separate companies continued in the trade and gave good service, the number growing less each year as they were replaced by steamers or became unserviceable.

It was the Albion ship DUNEDIN that pioneered the development of the frozen meat trade from New Zealand. In 1882, just prior to the amalgamation of the Albion Line with that of Shaw Savill, the DUNEDIN successfully carried the first cargo of frozen mutton and lamb from Port Chalmers to London. That cargo consisted of about 4,460 carcasses of mutton and 449 of lamb and the importance of the experiment can be judged by the fact that the majority of the Shaw Savill vessels prior to the introduction of containerisation had refrigerated capacity for some 250,000 carcasses, in addition to room for chilled cargo and large quantities of general cargo such as wool and milk powder.

About this time the White Star Line, hitherto trading only across the Atlantic, decided to enter the Australian and New Zealand trade and they agreed to run a combined service in conjunction with the Shaw Savill and Albion Company. White Star vessels so employed were identifiable by their wearing both house flags on the main and mizzen masts. For the service the White Star Line initially provided three vessels, the IONIC, DORIC and COPTIC and Shaw Savill the ARAWA and TAINUI, all fitted with refrigerating plant. These vessels each had a tonnage of about 5,000 gross tons, and were capable of a speed up to 15 knots. They made the outward voyage by way of Cape Town and Hobart to New Zealand, and homeward via Cape Horn and Rio de Janeiro, along the "Clipper" Way.

The time on passage from New Zealand was reduced from 90 – 100 days to 40 by the steamers, enabling them to "catch the market" in the U.K. On the route followed by the steamers, they frequently encountered heavy seas and it was not uncommon that they suffered the occasional broken propeller shaft.

This route was maintained up to the opening of the Panama Canal but in 1918 when commercial service was resumed after the First World War the direct route through the Panama Canal was used in both directions. Again, passage time was gradually reduced from the 74-100 days taken by the sailing ships, to less than 30 days for the WAIPAWA class of motor vessels in 1935.

The original five mail steamers were supplemented in 1889-1890 by the cargo vessels MAMARI, MAORI, MATATUA, RANGATIRA and PAKEHA. The original ARAWA, TAINUI, MAMARI, MATATUA, RANGATIRA and PAKEHA were later replaced by larger successors bearing the same names. The old ARAWA was fitted for 25,000 carcasses and the WAIMANA, built in 1911, was insulated for 100,000. It was not until 1913 that the last of the surviving sailing ships of the fleet, the HINEMOA was sold.

In the South African War of 1899-1902 Shaw Savill's vessels transported troops, explosives and horses from England and contingents of troops from New Zealand to South Africa.

In 1905 the Shaw Savill Line in conjunction with the White Star Line acquired a holding in the "Aberdeen Line" of Geo. Thompson & Co. Ltd., which had a notable record in the Australian trade dating back to 1825. At first this Australian connection was principally used to load ships out to Australia which could be used for homeward loading from New Zealand.

In the First World War of 1914-1918 although several ships of the fleet were attacked by submarines and some were damaged, only two became total losses through enemy action.

As time passed Shaw Savill became increasingly concerned in the Australian trade. In 1932, following a brief involvement with the Royal Mail Group, the Company acquired the fleet and assets of the Aberdeen Line. In April 1933 it also became manager and joint owner along with P. & O. of the newly formed Aberdeen and Commonwealth Line Ltd., which comprised the five BAY passenger steamers and the cargo steamer FORDSDALE, when the Australian Government sold them to British interests; complete ownership of this fleet was obtained in 1951. The passenger accommodation in the BAY steamers was completely remodelled and improved and they became very popular with Australians who preferred the One Class type of vessel.

A substantial share interest in Shaw Savill was acquired in 1933 by Furness Withy & Co. Ltd., this interest increased to almost the whole capital by the end of 1935.

In 1934, Shaw Savill purchased the Australian interests of the White Star Line, including the 18,481 ton passenger steamer CERAMIC.

During the same period, Shaw Savill took delivery of three 16.5 knot refrigerated motor vessels at a total cost of just over £1 million, intended for the Australia via Cape Town route. One, the WAIWERA, made a creditable run of 15 days, 14 hours and 12 minutes from Liverpool to Cape Town, thus bettering the time of contemporary Union-Castle mail vessels on the Southampton - Cape Town route.

An important addition to the fleet in 1939 was the DOMINION MONARCH, a quadruple-screw motor passenger and cargo vessel of around 27,000 tons with a speed of 19.5 knots. This vessel carried over 500 First class passengers and when launched was the largest vessel trading to New Zealand and the most powerful British motor ship. She inaugurated a new service to New Zealand via South Africa and Australia providing a direct link between Great Britain and her Dominions in the Southern Hemisphere.

The price paid by the Line during the Second World War of 1939-1945 was very heavy. Thirteen vessels - half of its fleet-were sunk. Three were lost in a single day (all of them among the latest and fastest motor vessels in the world), during the costliest of all the hard fought convoy battles to supply Malta, that of August 1942 known as "Operation Pedestal".

The sinking of the Aberdeen and Commonwealth liner JERVIS BAY on 5th November 1940 in action against the pocket battleship ADMIRAL SCHEER which attacked the convoy entrusted to her care, will long remain in history as one of the gallant epics of the War.

Shaw Savill & Albion was one of the founder members of the New Zealand Conference Lines. As early as 1873 Shaw Savill and Company had agreed along with the other two lines engaged in the New Zealand trade, the Albion Line and the New Zealand Shipping Co., on uniform freight rates. Later in 1879 Shaw Savill & Albion together with the New Zealand Shipping Company made a further agreement on the carriage of wool and mutton. The New Zealand Conference Overseas Shipowners' Committee founded in New Zealand in 1915 as a Government body in 1924 begat the Overseas Shipowners Allotment Committee, in which Shaw Savill was one of the original participants.

Following the Second World War, Shaw Savill was awarded £4 million compensation by the Government for its wartime losses. It was proposed that the immediate priorities for rebuilding the Shaw Savill fleet should be new cargo ships, the renovation of cargo-passenger ships, and new cargo-passenger ships. This was largely because most of the fleet were in their Autumn years, therefore a policy of not building passenger vessels until the cargo fleet had been brought up to strength was pursued. Existing passenger vessels (which, with the exception of the DOMINION MONARCH were between twenty and thirty-four years old), would be refurbished upon their release from Government service, by which time it was hoped that trends in post-war passenger traffic to the Antipodes would be clearly established. However, to meet the immediate requirements an order was placed in 1945 for one ship each with Harland & Wolff, Belfast, and Swan Hunter, Wallsend, and two at Cammell Laird of Birkenhead of a new cargo-passenger class of around 15,000 gross tons. These were later to become the ATHENIC, CORINTHIC, CERAMIC and GOTHIC respectively, while to initiate the programme Shaw Savill purchased the 12,829 gross ton EMPIRE GRACE which had been built for the Ministry of War Transport (M.o.W.T.) in 1942, to a Shaw Savill design and she was named the WAIRANGI.

During 1953–1954 the GOTHIC was chartered to convey the Queen and the Duke of Edinburgh on the Royal Commonwealth Tour originally planned for 1952 and postponed following the death of King George VI.

Changing conditions in cargo handling made it evident that it was unsatisfactory to carry large amounts of cargoes and passengers in the same vessel. To meet this specification of a purely passenger carrying ship with no cargo whatsoever, the 20,204 grt SOUTHERN CROSS entered service in 1955. Her design was unique as the machinery space was sited as far aft as was possible which gave more space and unobstructed decks to the 1,164 passengers carried. Most of the SOUTHERN CROSS's Public Rooms were air-conditioned and the vessel fitted with stabilisers. The absence of cargo enabled her to complete four round-the-world voyages a year and maintain a regular service. Seven years later in July 1962 the improved and larger NORTHERN STAR augmented the passenger service.

By 1967 the Company owned the largest fleet in its history, 35 ships which totalled some 402,239 gross tons. In this year and 1968 they took over three former Royal Mail liners and renamed them AKAROA, ARAWA and ARANDA. Together with the SOUTHERN CROSS and NORTHERN STAR and the cargo-passenger vessel CERAMIC, Shaw Savill then had the second largest British deep-sea passenger fleet with over 4,000 berths on offer.

The acquisition of the three ex-Royal Mail liners marked a return to the passenger-cargo vessel that Shaw Savill had decided against in the 1950s, and in fact the trio were destined never to pay their way under Shaw Savill ownership.

The 1970s saw the Company on the wane with many famous companies including themselves being rationalised under the Furness Withy holding group. Higher fuel costs, the introduction of containerisation in place of break-bulk cargo handling, and a massive decline of passenger traffic in favour of air travel all contributed to Shaw Savill's demise.

The NORTHERN STAR was disposed of in 1975 and ceased 125 years of passenger ship operation by Shaw Savill & Albion. The last ship owned by Shaw Savill was the containership DUNEDIN delivered in 1980, but by 1986 even she had been sold. The Furness Withy Group was itself taken over by the Orient Overseas Containers (Holdings) Ltd. of Hong Kong. Subsequently in October 1990 Furness Withy & Co. Ltd. was sold by OOCL to the German Company Hamburg-Sud for $130 million. The chosen name for the U.K. holding company was Shaw Savill Holdings Ltd.

NOTES TO THE ILLUSTRATIONS

1. Brief statistical particulars of the ships illustrated are incorporated in the Index on pages 139 to 143.

2. The author and publishers wish to thank the suppliers of the photographs used for permission to reproduce. Credits are shown in situ.

3. A Roman numeral following a ship's name indicates the first (second, etc) vessel of that name in the fleet.

4. Dates following the ship's name indicate the period during which the vessel concerned was owned or operated by the Shaw Savill Line.

5. The term "class" indicates that the ship in question is one of several ships of broadly similar design but subdivided into a number of smaller groups. The term "sister ship" indicates vessels built to the same dimensions, specifications, and power which are generally similar but not necessarily identical in appearance and layout.

6. For convenience and brevity the following abbreviations are used: The Shaw Savill & Albion Co.Ltd. = Shaw Savill.
Harland & Wolff Ltd. = Harland & Wolff.
Ministry of War Transport = M.o.W.T.
New Zealand = N.Z.

ZEALANDIA (1869–1902)

Built by C. Connell, Glasgow for Shaw Savill & Co., specially designed for the carriage of emigrants. 1877 Rammed and sunk the barque ELLEN LAMB. 1902 Completed a record of 33 round voyages to N.Z. 1903 Bought by Swedish owners. 1908 Renamed KALEVA. 1911 Stranded on the Northumbrian coast. 1919 Last recorded as a barge at St. John, New Brunswick.

DUNEDIN I (1882–1890)

1874 Built by Robert Duncan, Glasgow as one of the eight iron clipper ships for the Albion Line. February 1882 Selected as the pioneer ship of the New Zealand frozen meat trade and transported some 4931 carcasses to the U.K. with a passage time of 98 days. 1882 Taken over by Shaw Savill & Albion. 1890 Disappeared without trace whilst homeward bound from N.Z.

Sister ships: AUCKLAND, INVERCARGILL, WELLINGTON, CANTERBURY, NELSON, TIMARU, OAMARU.

CRUSADER (1869–1898) Tom Rayner Collection

1865 Built by C. Connell, Glasgow for John Lidgett & Sons. 1869 Purchased by Shaw Savill & Co. Made a record passage of 65 days from Lyttleton N.Z. to the English Channel. During her career, made 28 consecutive voyages to N.Z. and carried thousands of emigrants. 1898 Sold to Norwegian owners. 1910 Scrapped at Dordrecht.

MARGARET GALBRAITH (1876–1900)   Tom Rayner Collection

The first iron ship designed and built for the New Zealand trade. 1868 Built by Robert Duncan, Glasgow for the Albion Line and employed mainly on the Indian trade initially before being transferred to the New Zealand (N.Z.) run. 1876 Sold to Shaw Savill. 1900 Sold to Tasmanian owners. 25 March 1905 Wrecked en route from River Plate to U.K. on Farallon Reef.

LADY JOCELYN (1883–1889)

World Ship Society

1852 Built by C.J. Mare, London as an iron auxiliary screw-driven sailing vessel for the General Screw Shipping Co. 1854 Placed on the U.K. to Australia route via the Cape. 1855 Trooping to the Crimea and India and renamed BRAZIL. 1861 Resold and resumed name LADY JOCELYN. 1863 Carried troops from India to New Zealand for Maori War. 1883 Purchased by Shaw Savill & Albion and fitted with refrigerating machinery. 1889 Converted to a refrigeration hulk. 1899 Sold to the Shipping Federation. 1914–1918 Used as a floating barracks. 1922 Scrapped in Netherlands. Sister ship: HYDASPES.

"COPTIC.

COPTIC I (1884–1894)   Tom Rayner Collection

1881 Built by Harland & Wolff, Belfast for the White Star Line. On charter to Occidental & Oriental Steamship Co. 1884 Fitted with refrigeration machinery. 26 May Chartered by Shaw Savill & Albion for the London to N.Z. service via Cape town. 1894 Re-engined with triple expansion machinery. 1895 Resumed original San Fransisco - Hong Kong service. 1906 Purchased by Pacific Mail Steamship Co. and renamed PERSIA. 1915 Sold to Toyo Kisen Kaisha and renamed PERSIA MARU. 1926 Scrapped in Japan.
Sister ships: DORIC I, IONIC I.

IONIC I (1884–1899)

1883 Built by Harland & Wolff, Belfast for the White Star Line and chartered by the New Zealand Shipping Co. for the London to N.Z. service via Cape Town. 1884 Chartered by Shaw Savill & Albion for the same service. 1894 Re-engined with quadruple expansion machinery. 1900 sold to Aberdeen Line and renamed SOPHOCLES and used as a transport during the Boer War. 1908 Scrapped at Morecambe.
Sister ships. COPTIC I, DORIC I.
(Continued).

IONIC I (1884–1899) Tom Rayner Collection

Feb.1893 When outward bound from Cape Town, broke tail shaft. Towed back to Table Bay by the HAWARDEN CASTLE and following repairs resumed voyage to N.Z. This photo shows the IONIC after her 1894 refit with a taller funnel and square-rigged on the foremast only.

DORIC I (1884–1895)   Tom Rayner Collection

1883 Built by Harland & Wolff, Belfast for the White Star Line and chartered by the New Zealand Shipping Co. for the London to N.Z. service via Cape Town. 1884 Chartered by Shaw Savill & Albion for same service. May 1895 Re-engined with triple expansion machinery and transferred to the Occidental & Oriental Steamship Co. on the San Francisco-Hong Kong service. 1906 Purchased by Pacific Mail Steamship Co. and renamed ASIA. 23 April 1911 Wrecked on Finger Rock, Taichow Island, South China.
Sister ships: COPTIC I, IONIC I.

TAINUI I (1884–1899)   Shaw Savill Society

Built by Wm. Denny & Bros., Dumbarton. Along with the ARAWA built the same year was the first steamship built for Shaw Savill & Albion. 1896 Transferred to Spanish flag under charter to Spanish Government for trooping to Cuba. Renamed COVADONGA. 1898 Reverted to Shaw Savill. 1899 Sold to Allan Line and renamed ASTORIA. 1910 Sold to German ship breakers. 1911 Scrapped.
Sister ship: ARAWA I.
(Continued)

TAINUI I (1884–1899)   Tom Rayner Collection

The ARAWA and TAINUI were Shaw Savill's contribution to the joint steam service with the White Star Line. The names were taken from the legendary names of two of the principal canoes in which the Maoris made their migration to N.Z. The TAINUI is seen here in Allan Line funnel colours.

MAMARI I (1889–1903) World Ship Society

Built by Wm. Doxford & Sons, Sunderland. Nick-named the "New Zealand thief" on account of a large insulated capacity of 136,640 cubic feet. 1899 Whilst rounding Cape Horn, the tail shaft broke during a gale. Towed to Montevideo by the steamer GULF OF CORCOVADO. 1903 Sold to Houston Line and renamed HESIONE. 1915 Sunk by submarine U41, 86 miles S.E. of Fastnet.
Sister ship: OTARAMA (N.Z.S.Co)

RANGATIRA I (1890–1909) Tom Rayner Collection

Built by Wm. Gray & Co., West Hartlepool. 1909 Sold to the Vestey organisation and renamed GRAF MURAVIEFF under the Russian flag for use in the Siberian salmon fisheries. 1911 Transferred to Blue Star under British registry and renamed BRODMORE. 27 February 1917 Topedoed and sunk by a German submarine 70 miles N.W. of Marsa Susa in the Mediterranean.
Sister ship: PAKEHA I.

LINDFIELD I (1891–1911)
Tom Rayner Collection

Built by Russell & Co., Greenock as a steel 4–masted barque for the carriage of general cargo in Walter Savill's Company.
1911 Sold to Norwegian owners. 1916 Torpedoed and sunk by a German U-boat off Southern Ireland.
Sister ships: HINEMOA, MAYFIELD I.

MAYFIELD I (1892–1905)
Tom Rayner Collection

Built by Russell & Co., Greenock as a steel 4–masted barque for the carriage of general cargo in Walter Savill's Company.
5 February 1905 Wrecked on the Tasmanian coast off Swan Island without loss of life.
Sister ships: HINEMOA, LINDFIELD I.

GOTHIC I (1893–1907)

Built by Harland & Wolff, Belfast for the White Star Line. Entered the joint Shaw Savill service from London to N.Z. via Cape Town. The first twin-screw ship to sail to N.Z. with accommodation for 104 First and 114 Third class passengers. June 1906 Beached at Plymouth after being damaged by fire. 1907 Transferred to Red Star Line and renamed GOTHLAND. 1911 Reverted to White Star and renamed GOTHIC. 1913 Reverted to GOTHLAND. 1914 Stranded near Scilly Isles. 1926 Scrapped at Bo'ness, sold for £16,000.

TOKOMARU (1893–1915)

World Ship Society

Built by C.S. Swan & Hunter, Wallsend as the WESTMEATH with a refrigerated capacity of 250,000 cubic feet. Renamed TOKOMARU by Shaw Savill and capable of carrying 85,000 carcasses. September 1897, Whilst homeward bound from N.Z. in the South Atlantic tail shaft broke; she continued 600 miles under sail to Rio where repairs were effected. 1901 Called at St. Helena with supplies for Boer P.o.Ws. 30 January 1915 Torpedoed and sunk 7 miles N.W. of Le Havre by German U-boat U20.
Sister ship: AOTEA.

WAIWERA I (1898–1926)   A. Duncan

Built by Wm. Denny & Bros., Dumbarton with a cargo capacity for 80,000 carcasses. 1899 On 1st October sailed from Wellington with the first contingent of New Zealand troops to fight in the Boer War. 1917 Torpedo fired from a German U-boat missed while WAIWERA was off the Lizard. 1926 Sold to Ellerman Bucknall Line and renamed CITY OF PRETORIA. 1928 Sold for £11,000 and scrapped at Barrow.
Sister ship: KUMARA I.

KUMARA I (1899–1927) World Ship Society

Built by C.S. Swan & Hunter, Wallsend with cargo capacity for 75,000 carcasses. 1899 Used as a troopship during the Boer War. Entered London to N.Z. service via Cape Town. 1914–18 Requisitioned under the Liner Requisition Scheme. 1927 Sold to Swedish owners for £14,000. 1928 Scrapped at Venice.
Sister ship: WAIWERA I.

ATHENIC I (1901–1928)   Tom Rayner Collection

Built by Harland & Wolff, Belfast for the White Star Line/Shaw Savill joint service. She was especially designed along with her sister ships for the carriage of frozen cargo in addition to a large number of passengers. 1916 Embarked British P.o.Ws. captured by the German raider MOEWE at Santa Cruz. 1920 Rescued part of the crew of American steamer MUNAMAR. 1928 Sold to Norwegians and converted to Whale factory ship PELAGOS. 1962 Scrapped in Germany. Sister ships: CORINTHIC I, IONIC II.
(Continued)

ATHENIC I (1901–1928)   John Clarkson

A photo of the ATHENIC in her later years with an enclosed wheelhouse and additional lifeboats. The Shaw Savill houseflag may be clearly seen flying from the mizzen mast while White Star's is atop the mainmast.

IONIC II (1902–1936)

Built by Harland & Wolff, Belfast for the White Star Line/ Shaw Savill joint service. 16 January 1903 Maiden voyage from London to Wellington via Cape Town. 1909 The first ship trading to N.Z. to be fitted with wireless telegraphy. 1914–18 Transport work, later requisitioned under the Liner Requisition Scheme. 31 January 1919 Resumed service to N.Z. via Panama Canal. 1927 Rescued crew of French vessel DAISY off the Grand Banks. 1932 Transferred to Shaw Savill & Albion and reconstructed for Tourist class only. 1937 Scrapped in Japan.
Sister ships: CORINTHIC I, ATHENIC I.

CORINTHIC I (1902–1931)

Built by Harland & Wolff, Belfast for the White Star Line/Shaw Savill joint service. 20 November 1902 Maiden voyage from London to N.Z. via Cape Town. 1917 Requisitioned under the Liner Requisition Scheme. 1920 Resumed service to N.Z. via Panama Canal. 1923 Rescued crew of Newfoundland schooner MARGUERITE RYAN. 1926 Outward bound to N.Z. raced with N.Z.S.Co. REMUERA. 1931 Scrapped at Wallsend.
Sister ships: ATHENIC I, IONIC II.

MAMARI II (1904–1928)   World Ship Society

Built by Harland & Wolff, Belfast. The first steamer to be built by Harland & Wolff for Shaw Savill. November 1906 Whilst being drydocked at Auckland shifted on the keel blocks causing a large wave which killed two workmen. 1910 Made a record round-the-world voyage of just over three months, between March and June. 1928 Sold to Arnold Bernstein of Germany and renamed GEROLSTEIN, 1939 Sold to H.C. Horn (German). Renamed CONSUL HORN. 20 July 1942 Mined and sunk off Borkum.
Sister ship: MATATUA II.

MATATUA II (1904–1928)   A. Duncan

Built by Workman, Clark & Co., Belfast. At the time the MATATUA was reputed to have the tallest funnel of any ship in the world. 1916 Serious fire on board whilst in Canadian waters; the Master was killed. 1928 Sold to Arnold Bernstein of Germany and renamed ILSENSTEIN. 1939 Sold. 1940 Sunk as a blockship at Scapa Flow. 1950 Cut up for scrap. Sister ship: MAMARI II.

KIA ORA (1907–1935)   Shaw Savill Society

Built by Workman, Clark & Co., Belfast. The vessel had a reasonably good speed for its era. She made many fast passages howeward round Cape Horn to deliver on time to the London wool sales. 1935 Sold to Italian owners and renamed VERBANIA. July 1940 Taken over by British as a war prize at Haifa and renamed EMPIRE TAMAR for M.o.W.T. June 1944 Scuttled as a blockship at the Normandy beachhead (Gooseberry No.5).

R.M.S. ARAWA.

PROTECTED BY J. 08
ALDERSLEY SER...

ARAWA II (1907–1928)

A. Duncan

Built by Swan Hunter & Wigham Richardson, Wallsend. Constructed especially for the frozen meat trade with passenger accommodation for 220 in three classes. 1909 Lost starboard screw after leaving Cape Town, so continued the voyage to Wellington at 9.5 knots on the remaining propeller. 1914–15 Employed on troopship duties. 1921 Resumed service to N.Z. via Panama Canal. 1926 Converted to a Cabin class ship. 1928 Sold to Arnold Bernstein of Germany and renamed KONIGSTEIN. 1939 Sold to Cie Maritime Belge and renamed GANDIA. 22 January 1942 Torpedoed and sunk in mid-Atlantic, N.W. of Azores, by U-135.
Sister ship: TAINUI II.

TAINUI II (1908–1939) Tom Rayner Collection

Built by Workman, Clark & Co., Belfast. 1913 Collided with steamer INCA. 1917 Requisitioned under the Liner Requisition Scheme. 1921 Resumed service to N.Z. via Panama Canal. 1932 Converted to Tourist class only. 1939 Sold to shipbreakers. 1940 Resold to M.o.W.T. and renamed EMPIRE TRADER; managed by Shaw Savill & Albion. 21 February 1943 Torpedoed by a submarine in the North Atlantic, later sank.
Sister ship: ARAWA II.

RANGATIRA II (1909–1916) Tom Rayner Collection

Built by Workman, Clark & Co. Belfast. The first of many of the Company's ships to be designed by Shaw Savill Master, Captain R.J. Noal. 1916 Grounded at Robben Island, Table Bay when en route to Tasmania and N.Z. Abandoned as Constructive Total Loss.

PAKEHA II (1910–1939, 1946–1950)

Built by Harland & Wolff, Belfast. 1917 Requisitioned under the Liner Requisition Scheme. 1939 Sold to the Admiralty and camouflaged as H.M.S. REVENGE. Transferred to M.o.W.T. and refitted as a refrigerated cargo vessel. Renamed EMPIRE PAKEHA and managed by Shaw Savill. 1946 Repurchased by Shaw Savill and renamed PAKEHA. 1950 Scrapped at Briton Ferry.
(Continued).

PAKEHA II (1910–1939, 1946–1950)   M. Condie
PAKEHA is the Maori word for White man. She was distinguished by a tall funnel to produce natural draught for her boilers. Provision for 1000 emigrant passengers.

WAIMANA (1911–1926, 1932–1939, 1944–1952)　　　　　　　　　Tom Rayner Collection

Built by Workman Clark & Co., Belfast. Designed with insulated space for 100,000 carcasses and with accommodation for First and Steerage class passengers. 1915 Diverted to South American meat trade for a number of voyages. 1917 Requisitioned under the Liner Requisition Scheme. 1926 Transferred to the Aberdeen Line and renamed HERMINIUS. (Continued).

41

Tom Rayner Collection

HERMINIUS (1926–1932)

Shaw Savill's WAIMANA as the HERMINIUS on charter to George Thompson's Aberdeen Line. 1932 Returned to Shaw Savill and renamed WAIMANA. 1939 Sold to the Admiralty and camouflaged as H.M.S. RESOLUTION. 1941 Transferred to M.o.W.T. and refitted as a refrigerated cargo vessel. Renamed EMPIRE WAIMANA. (Continued).

A. Duncan

EMPIRE WAIMANA (1941–1946)

Although owned by the M.o.W.T. she was managed by Shaw Savill. 1946 Repurchased by Shaw Savill and renamed WAIMANA. 1952 Scrapped at Milford Haven.

ZEALANDIC I (1911–1926)

Tom Rayner Collection

Built by Harland & Wolff, Belfast, for White Star Line/Shaw Savill joint service. 1913 Chartered by Western Australia Government for emigrant duties. 1917 Requisitioned under the Liner Requisition Scheme. 1923 Assisted the disabled sailing ship GARTHSNAID near Cape Howe and towed her into Melbourne. 1926 Transferred to the Aberdeen Line and renamed MAMILIUS.
(Continued).

MAMILIUS (1926–1932)

Shaw Savill's ZEALANDIC spent six years as the MAMILIUS. Along with the WAIMANA she was chartered to George Thompson's Aberdeen Line. 1932 Returned to Shaw Savill and renamed MAMARI. An early view of the MAMARI. (Continued).

MAMARI III (1932–1939)　　　　　　　　　　　　　　　　　　　　　　　J.K. Byass

The former ZEALANDIC was returned to Shaw Savill and operated for seven years as the MAMARI. 1939 Sold to the **Admiralty and camouflaged** to represent the aircraft carrier H.M.S. HERMES. 3 June 1941 Whilst proceeding to Chatham **Dockyard to be reconverted** to a refrigerated cargo ship, she struck the wreck of the tanker AHAMO about 30 miles north **of Wells, (Norfolk).** 10 June 1941 Torpedoed whilst aground by E-Boat and abandoned as a total loss.

RARANGA (1916–1950)

A. Duncan

Built by Armstrong Whitworth & Co. Ltd., Newcastle. Constructed as a cargo only vessel with a refrigerated capacity of well over 350,000 cubic feet. Very similar in appearance to the PAKEHA and identified by her tall funnel. 1950 Scrapped at Blyth.

A. Duncan

MAHANA (1917–1953)

Built by Workman Clark & Co. Ltd., Belfast. Constructed to the design of Captain Noal, then Shaw Savill marine superintendent at the time and was the first turbine-driven vessel built for the Company. 1917 On completion, requisitioned under the Liner Requisition Scheme. Capable of carrying 1,500 emigrants. c 1926 Passenger accommodation removed. 1950 Requisitioned by the Ministry of Food as a floating store ship. 1953 Scrapped at Dalmuir.

MAHIA (1917–1953) A. Duncan

Built by Workman Clark & Co., Belfast. Along with the MAHANA she was one of the last coal-burners on the N.Z. trade. 1939 Laid up. 1939–45 Employed mainly on commercial service. 1947 Cargo caught fire whilst at Melbourne. Repairs cost £100,000. 1948 Resumed service. 1953 Scrapped at Faslane. Her withdrawal marked the end of the coalburning era of the Company.

OTIRA (1919–1936)

Tom Rayner Collection

Built by Harland & Wolff, Belfast as the WAR PARIS for H.M. Shipping Controller. 1919 Collided in the River Thames whilst in fog. 1936 Laid up in the Gareloch. Scrapped in Italy.
Sister ship: KUMARA II. (63)

TAIROA (1920–1939)

Built by Armstrong Whitworth & Co., Newcastle, as a cargo-only vessel. 3 December 1939 Sunk in the South Atlantic by the German pocket battleship ADMIRAL GRAF SPEE.
Sister ship: MAIMOA

MAIMOA (1920–1940)   W.S.S. Southampton, Hartwell Bequest

Built by Palmers' Co. Ltd., Newcastle as a cargo-only vessel. 20 November 1940 Sunk by German raider PINGUIN in the Indian Ocean.
Sister ship: TAIROA.

ZEALANDIC II (1928–1941)

Built by Swan Hunter & Wigham Richardson, Wallsend. Shaw Savill's first motorship. Accommodation for 8 passengers and insulated capacity of over 400,000 cubic feet. 20 January 1941 Whilst on passage from Liverpool to Australia, torpedoed and sunk by a German U-boat 450 miles south of the Westman Islands. 74 lives were lost.
Sister ships: COPTIC II, KARAMEA II, TARANAKI.

TARANAKI (1928–1963)

World Ship Photo Library

Built by Fairfield Shipbuilding & Engineering Co., Ltd. Glasgow. Accommodation for 8 passengers, later reduced to 6. 1950 Collided with Union S.S.Co. WAIPIATA in Wellington Heads. 1955 Extensively refitted with passenger space refurbished for officers. 1963 Scrapped at Aioi, Japan.
Sister ships: ZEALANDIC II, COPTIC II, KARAMEA II.
(Continued).

TARANAKI (1928–1963)

World Ship Photo Library

A wartime view of the TARANAKI in grey livery as a D.E.M.S. The photograph dates the time taken 13 October 1943, possibly somewhere in American waters.

COPTIC II (1928–1965) World Ship Photo Library

Built by Swan Hunter & Wigham Richardson, Wallsend. Accommodation for 8 passengers, later reduced to 6. The choice of COPTIC broke with Shaw Savill's tradition of giving their vessels Maori names. 1955 Extensive refit in which passenger space was refurbished for officers. The COPTIC gave the Company 37 years of reliable service. 1965 Scrapped in Antwerp. Sister ships: KARAMEA II, TARANAKI, ZEALANDIC II.

KARAMEA II (1928–1960)   F.R. Sherlock

Built by Fairfield Shipbuilding & Engineering Co., Ltd. Glasgow. October 1939 First Shaw Savill vessel attacked by enemy in World War II. Shelled by surfaced German submarine but evaded being hit. 1941 Attacked and bombed by enemy aircraft; hit by a bomb which failed to explode. Later refitted and refrigerated capacity increased. 1960 Inaugurated a cargo service between N.Z., South Africa and West African ports. December 1960 Scrapped by T.W. Ward, Inverkeithing. Sister ships: COPTIC II, TARANAKI, ZEALANDIC II.

THEMISTOCLES (1932–1947)

1911 Built by Harland & Wolff, Belfast for the Aberdeen Line. 1932 Transferred to Shaw Savill. Employed on the Australian service from Liverpool via Cape Town. 1946 Laid up in the River Blackwater. 1947 Scrapped at Dalmuir.

Akaroa : a Shaw Savill and Albion passenger liner in Akaroa Harbour, N.Z.

AKAROA II (1932–1954)   Shaw Savill Line

1914 Built by Harland & Wolff, Belfast as the EURIPIDES for the Aberdeen Line. 1932 Transferred to Shaw Savill and renamed AKAROA. Given an extensive refit on the Tyne before entering the Southampton to N.Z. service via Panama. 1946 Following War commercial service reconditioned at Wallsend as a Cabin class ship for 198 passengers. 1947 Resumed London to N.Z. service via Panama. 1954 Scrapped at Antwerp.

TAMAROA (1932–1957)

1922 Built by Harland & Wolff, Belfast as the SOPHOCLES for the Aberdeen Line. 1926 Chartered by Shaw Savill and renamed TAMAROA and converted to burn oil fuel. 1931 Third class accommodation removed. 1932 Transferred to Shaw Savill. 1940 Troop transport. 1948 Resumed London to N.Z. service via Panama. 1957 Scrapped at Blyth. Sister ship: MATAROA.

MATAROA (1932–1957)

1922 Built by Harland & Wolff, Belfast as the DIOGENES for the Aberdeen Line. 1926 Chartered by Shaw Savill and renamed MATAROA. 1926 Converted to burn oil fuel and entered Southampton to N.Z. service via Panama. 1931 Third class accommodation removed. 1932 Transferred to Shaw Savill. 1940 Troop transport. 1948 Resumed London to N.Z. service via Panama. 1957 Scrapped at Faslane.
Sister ship: TAMAROA.

FORDSDALE (1932–1952)

Tom Rayner Collection

1924 Built by Commonwealth Dockyard, Sydney, Australia for the Aberdeen & Commonwealth Line. 1932 Taken over by Shaw Savill. 1952 Sold and renamed OCEAN NEPTUNE. 1954 Renamed PACIFIC TRADER. 1956 Renamed ATLANTIC CONCORD (Pan). 1958 JUI YUNG (China Nat.) 1959 Scrapped in Japan.
Sister ship: FERNDALE.

KUMARA II (1933–1937)   Tom Rayner Collection

1918 Built by Harland & Wolff, Belfast as the WAR PRIAM for H.M. Shipping Controller. 1919 Purchased by White Star and renamed BARDIC. 1925 Transferred to Aberdeen Line and renamed HORATIUS. 1933 Acquired by Shaw Savill and renamed KUMARA. 1936 Laid up at Gareloch. 1937 Sold to Marathon S.S. Co. and renamed MARATHON. 9 March 1941 Sunk by the German battle cruiser SCHARNHORST N.E. of Cape Verde Islands. The photo shows the KUMARA laid up in the Gareloch on 27 July 1936.
Sister ship: OTIRA (50)

MORETON BAY (1933–1957)

1921 Built by Vickers Ltd., Barrow-in-Furness for the Aberdeen & Commonwealth Line. Accommodation for 514 passengers. Entered London to Australia service via Suez. 1933 Part-owned by Shaw Savill. 1939 Requisitioned as an Armed Merchant Cruiser. 1941 Converted to a troopship. 1948 Resumed London to Australia service via Suez and Colombo. 1951. Wholly owned by Shaw Savill. 1957 Scrapped at Barrow.
Sister ships: LARGS BAY, HOBSONS BAY, ESPERANCE BAY (later ARAWA), JERVIS BAY.

HOBSONS BAY (1933–1936)/ESPERANCE BAY II (1936–55)   A.Duncan

1922 Built by Vickers Ltd., Barrow-in-Furness as the HOBSONS BAY for the Aberdeen & Commonwealth Line. Accommodation for 514 passengers. Entered London to Australia service via Suez. 1933 Part-owned by Shaw Savill. 1936 Renamed ESPERANCE BAY. 1939 Requisitioned as an Armed Merchant Cruiser. 1941 Converted to a troopship. 1948 Resumed London to Australia service via Suez and Colombo. 1951 Wholly owned by Shaw Savill. 1955 Scrapped at Faslane.
Sister ships: MORETON BAY, LARGS BAY, ESPERANCE BAY I (later ARAWA), JERVIS BAY.

JERVIS BAY (1933–1940)

A. Duncan

1922 Built by Vickers Ltd., Barrow-in-Furness, for the Aberdeen & Commonwealth Line. Original accommodation for 723 passengers. Entered London to Australia service via Suez. 1933 Part-owned by Shaw Savill. 1939 Commandeered as an Armed Merchant Cruiser. 5 November 1940 Sunk by gunfire by the German naval vessel ADMIRAL SCHEER, in the North Atlantic.

Sister ships: MORETON BAY, LARGS BAY, HOBSONS BAY (ESPERANCE BAY II), ESPERANCE BAY I (later ARAWA).

LARGS BAY (1933–1957)　　　　　　　　　　　　　　　　　Tom Rayner Collection

1921 Built by Wm. Beardmore & Co., Glasgow for the Aberdeen & Commonwealth Line. Accommodation for 514 passengers. 1922 Entered London to Australia service via Suez. 1933 Part-owned by Shaw Savill. 1941 Converted to a troopship. 1948–49 Refitted and resumed London to Australia service via Suez and Colombo. 1951 Wholly owned by Shaw Savill. 1957 Scrapped at Barrow.
Sister ships: MORETON BAY, HOBSONS BAY, ESPERANCE BAY I (later ARAWA), JERVIS BAY.

ARAWA III (1936–1955)   Tom Rayner Collection

1922 Built by Wm. Beardmore & Co., Glasgow as the ESPERANCE BAY for the Aberdeen & Commonwealth Line. Original accommodation for 723 passengers. 1933 Part-owned by Shaw Savill. 1936 Transferred to Shaw Savill and renamed ARAWA. 1936–37 Refitted on the Clyde, and entered Southampton to N.Z. service via Panama. 1939 Requisitioned as an Armed Merchant Cruiser. 1941 Converted to a troopship. 1946 Resumed London to N.Z. service via Cape Town. 1955 Scrapped at Newport, Mon.
Sister ships: MORETON BAY, LARGS BAY, HOBSONS BAY, JERVIS BAY.

A. Duncan

WAIWERA II (1934–1942)
Built by Harland & Wolff, Belfast. The first of a class of 3 new large refrigerated vessels or "Empire Food Ships", with a capacity for 150,000 carcasses of mutton. Accommodation for 12 passengers. 1935 Made a record passage to Cape Town of 15 days, 14 hours and 12 minutes. 29 June 1942 Torpedoed and sunk in the Atlantic.
Sister ships: WAIPAWA, WAIRANGI I, WAIMARAMA, (81) WAIOTIRA.

M.V. "WAIPAWA."

WAIPAWA (1934–1967)   B.A. Feilden

Built by Harland & Wolff, Belfast. Accommodation for 12 passengers, refrigerated capacity of over 500,000 cubic feet. Together with the WAIWERA and WAIRANGI cost around £1 million. 1945 Only one of five sisters to survive World War II. 1967 Sold and renamed ARAMIS (Greek). 1968 Scrapped in Taiwan.
Sister ships: WAIWERA II, WAIRANGI I, WAIMARAMA, (81) WAIOTIRA.

M.V. "WAIRANGI"

WAIRANGI I (1935–1942)

Built by Harland & Wolff, Glasgow. Accommodation for 12 passengers. 13 August 1942 Whilst on the Pedestal convoy to Malta, torpedoed and sunk in the Mediterranean.
Sister ships: WAIWERA II, WAIPAWA, WAIMARAMA, (81) WAIOTIRA.

CERAMIC I (1934–1940)   Tom Rayner Collection

1913 Built by Harland & Wolff for White Star Line's Australian service. For many years was the largest liner operating on this route. 1934 Following Cunard's merger with White Star was transferred to Shaw Savill. Operated on the Liverpool to Australia via Cape Town route. 1936 Modernised by Harland & Wolff, Glasgow. 1940 Damaged in collision with Bank Line vessel TESTBANK. 6 December 1942 Torpedoed and sunk by German submarine U515 in the North Atlantic.

S. S. "Corinthic".
(Twin Screw).
12,231 tons.

CORINTHIC I (1902–1931)

A Retouched colour "Maoriland Postcard" published by Tanner Bros. of Wellington (N.Z.) and printed in Saxony. It is not known whether this type of card was sold on the ships or not.

Shaw Savill & Albion Co Ltd.   R.M.S. "TAMAROA."   Gatun Lake, Panama Canal.

TAMAROA (1932–1957)

A popular vessel on the New Zealand passenger trade with a capacity for 367.

Alan Mallett Collection

COPTIC II (1928–1965)   A.C. Reed
A previously unpublished post-war photo of the COPTIC. She was one of the first motorships built for Shaw Savill.

DOMINION MONARCH (1939–1962)   A.C. Reed

The DOMINION MONARCH, photographed by one of her former officers back in 1958, whilst berthed in New Zealand.

CERAMIC II (1948–1972)

A.C.Reed

The CERAMIC in Wellington back in 1958.

NEW AUSTRALIA (1950–1957)
The specially reconstructed liner which transported the "£10 Poms" of the 1950s to their new life in Australia.

Gladstone-Hornby Lock and docks to the southward.

CEDRIC (1952–1976)   Author's Collection
The CEDRIC transiting the Gladstone-Hornby Lock at Liverpool. Note that she is in a light-loaded condition, probably after discharge of cargo.

NORTHERN STAR (1962–1975)   W.H. Mitchell

A good view taken of the NORTHERN STAR showing her distinctive funnel markings.

WAIMARAMA (1938–1942)

A. Duncan

Built by Harland & Wolff, Belfast. The Company's first vessel to employ the newly designed H&W "coverless" engine. It was rumoured that her top speed was 20 knots. Remained on regular commercial service until 1940. 13 August 1942 Whilst on the Pedestal convoy to Malta, bombed and sunk in the Mediterranean. This photo shows the WAIMARAMA on commercial service leaving Cape Town.

Sister ships: WAIWERA II (69), WAIPAWA (70), WAIRANG I (71) WAIOTIRA.

1292 C. R. Hoffmann. Southampton. SHAW SAVILL & ALBION CO'S DOMINION MONARCH. 26,500 Tons.

DOMINION MONARCH (1939–1962)

C.R. Hoffmann

Built by Swan Hunter & Wigham Richardson, Wallsend. The largest passenger ship ever owned by Shaw Savill, and the largest vessel built on the Tyne since Cunard's MAURETANIA of 1907. This well known post card has been suspiciously touched up showing the newly delivered liner with a false bow wave.
(Continued).

DOMINION MONARCH · DINING SALOON

DOMINION MONARCH (1939–1962)

Shaw Savill Society

The Dining Saloon extended the full width of the ship with very large side windows and gave the impression of spaciousness.
A system of air-conditioning maintained an even temperature in all climates and contributed to the passengers' comfort.
(Continued).

DOMINION MONARCH . DRAWING ROOM

DOMINION MONARCH (1939–1962)

Shaw Savill Society

The Drawing Room's decoration was in the "Adam" style. The panelling was of natural pine, with eighteenth century furniture in mahogany upholstered in rich brocatelle and damasks. The satin curtains were of a soft peach colour. (Continued).

DOMINION MONARCH — GAMES DECK

DOMINION MONARCH (1939–1962)

Shaw Savill Society

The Games Deck had a length of 250 feet and, with the lifeboats stowed well above the deck a full width of 86.5 feet was available for sports such deck tennis and deck golf.
(Continued).

DOMINION MONARCH . THE LOUNGE

DOMINION MONARCH (1939–1962)   Shaw Savill Society

The Lounge. This public room with its large armchairs and luxurious carpet had a centre floor available for dancing. The panelling was Canadian block elm.
(Continued).

DOMINION MONARCH · SMOKE ROOM

DOMINION MONARCH (1939–1962)

Shaw Savill Society

The Smoke Room was sixteenth century in style giving the impression of a Tudor mansion. The ceiling was oak beamed and the ingle-nook was of rough plaster with its broad stone chimney piece and red brick hearth. (Continued).

DOMINION MONARCH · VERANDA AND CINEMA

DOMINION MONARCH (1939–1962)

Shaw Savill Society

The Verandah and Cinema was an attractive place for passengers to sit especially in the warmer latitudes, with its Lloyd-loom coloured cane furniture and flowering shrubs.
(Continued).

DOMINION MONARCH (1939–1962)

Shaw Savill Line

1939 Entered the Southampton to Australia and N.Z. service via Cape Town. 1940 Requisitioned as a troopship. She is seen here in wartime livery. The **DOMINION MONARCH** nearly became a casualty of war during a refit in Singapore Dockyard, shortly before the fall of that Island to the Japanese. (Continued).

DOMINION MONARCH (1939–1962)

Tom Rayner Collection

1948 Resumed the service from London to Australia and N.Z. via Cape Town. 1962 Sold for £400,000 and used as a hotel ship at the Seattle World Fair. 1962 Renamed DOMINION MONARCH MARU. Scrapped at Osaka, Japan.

WAIWERA III (1944–1967)

M. Windsor-Smith

Built by Harland & Wolff, Belfast, based on the 1934 WAIWERA II design, with wartime emergency accommodation for 100 passengers. Notable for being one of only 4 vessels fitted with the newly designed H&W built, Opposed-Piston diesel engine, not previously tested in service, and regrettably overlooked by maritime historians. 1950 Passenger accommodation reduced to 12. 1963 Mutiny aboard whilst in Royal Albert Dock. 1967 Sold and renamed JULIA (Greek). 1968 Scrapped at Kaohsiung, Taiwan.

WAIRANGI II (1946–1963) World Ship Photo Library

1942 Built by Harland & Wolff, Belfast as the EMPIRE GRACE for the M.o.W.T. Emergency built wartime cargo vessel, based on the WAIMARAMA design, but operated and managed by Shaw Savill. Accommodation for 112 passengers. 1946 Bought by Shaw Savill and renamed WAIRANGI. 1951 Passenger accommodation removed. 1963 Grounded at the Island of Kloevholmen near Stockholm. 1963 Scrapped at Faslane.
Sister ships: EMPIRE HOPE, EMPIRE MERCIA, EMPIRE WESSEX.

CORINTHIC II (1947–1969)

Shaw Savill Line

Built by Cammell Laird & Co., Birkenhhead. 1947 Whilst under construction fire aboard delayed completion. 1947 Entered Liverpool to Australia and N.Z service via South Africa and return via Panama. The Company's first post-war passenger vessel, known as the "Big IC" class. Normally employed on the London to N.Z. route via Panama. 1965 Passenger accommodation removed. 1969 Scrapped at Kaohsiung, Taiwan.
Sister ships: ATHENIC II, CERAMIC II, GOTHIC II.

F.R. Sherlock

ATHENIC II (1947–1969)
Built by Harland & Wolff, Belfast. Entered London to N.Z service via Panama. 1965 Passenger accommodation removed.
1969 Scrapped at Kaohsiung, Taiwan.
Sister ships: CORINTHIC II, CERAMIC II, GOTHIC II.

CERAMIC II (1948–1972)

F.R. Sherlock

Built by Cammell Laird & Co., Birkenhead. Entered Liverpool to N.Z. service via Panama. After maiden voyage sailed out of London. 1954 High pressure turbine removed and installed into GOTHIC while latter was on Royal Tour. 1968 Only vessel of the four post-war sisters to retain its passenger accommodation after the others had been derated to cargo-only vessels. 1972 Scrapped at Tamise in Belgium.
Sister ships: ATHENIC II, CORINTHIC II, GOTHIC II.

GOTHIC II (1948–1969)   Tom Rayner Collection

Built by Swan Hunter & Wigham Richardson, Wallsend. 1948 Entered Liverpool to N. Z. service via Panama. After maiden voyage sailed out of London. 1953–54 Chartered as Royal Yacht for the Queen's World Tour. 1954 Resumed normal service. 1968 Fire aboard when 5 days out of N.Z., 7 fatalities. Passenger accommodation closed. 1969 Scrapped at Kaohsiung, Taiwan. This view was taken in 1957.
Sister ships: ATHENIC II, CORINTHIC II, CERAMIC II.
(Continued).

GOTHIC II (1948–1969)

A. Duncan

Here the GOTHIC is seen in the livery as a Royal Yacht. The GOTHIC was chartered at a cost of £825,000.

PERSIC (1949–1969)

W.S.S. Southampton, Hartwell Bequest

Built by Cammell Laird & Co., Birkenhead at a cost of £1.5 million. First of a trio of vessels similar to the "Big IC" class but without passenger accommodation. 1969 Transferred to Royal Mail and renamed DERWENT. 1971 Scrapped in Spain.
Sister ships: RUNIC, SUEVIC.

DORIC II (1949–1969)

J.K. Byass

Built by Fairfield Shipbuilding & Engineering Co., Glasgow. First of the Company's post W.W.2 vessels to have Doxford diesel engines installed since the DOMINION MONARCH of 1939. 1969 Scrapped at Tamise in Belgium. Sister ship: DELPHIC.

DELPHIC (1949–1971)

Built by Hawthorn Leslie & Co. Ltd., Newcastle. The first Shaw Savill vessel to be built at this shipyard since the screw steamer KARAMEA I of 1899. 1971 Scrapped at Kaohsiung, Taiwan.
Sister ship: DORIC II.

RUNIC (1950–1961)

Built by Harland & Wolff, Belfast. Completed only 21 voyages during her brief career with the Company. 1961 Stranded on Middleton Reef whilst en route to North Island N.Z. from Brisbane. Declared a constructive total loss.
Sister ships: PERSIC, SUEVIC.

SUEVIC (1950–1974)   A. Duncan

Built by Harland & Wolff, Belfast. 1968 Small fire in cargo of whisky, whilst discharging at Sydney. A very popular ship with former crew members. 1969 Laid up in River Blackwater. 1974 Scrapped at Kaohsiung, Taiwan.
Sister ships: PERSIC, RUNIC.

NEW AUSTRALIA (1950–1957)

1931 Built by Vickers-Armstrongs Ltd., Newcastle for Furness Withy & Co. Ltd. as MONARCH OF BERMUDA. 1947 Caught fire during refit on the Tyne and severely damaged. Purchased by the Ministry of Transport and rebuilt as an emigrant carrier. This photograph, source unidentified, shows work in progress.
(Continued).

NEW AUSTRALIA (1950–1957)

Tom Rayner Collection

1948 Conversion to carry 1583 passengers completed by John I. Thornycroft Ltd., Southampton, at a cost of £3 million.
1950 Renamed NEW AUSTRALIA and manned and managed by Shaw Savill. Entered Southampton to Australia service via Suez.
(Continued).

SHAW SAVILL LINER "NEW AUSTRALIA"
RECONSTRUCTED BY JOHN THORNYCROFT & Co. Ltd., SOUTHAMPTON

20,256 Tons

NEW AUSTRALIA (1950–1957)

O.W. Hoffmann

This photograph clearly shows the coat-of-arms of the Commonwealth of Australia on her bows. Her reconstruction involved the use of more than 3,000 tons of steel. She also served as a troopship during the Korean War and Suez campaign. 1958 Sold to Greek Line and renamed ARKADIA. 1966 Broken up in Spain.
Sister ship: QUEEN OF BERMUDA.

CEDRIC (1952–1976)

Tom Rayner Collection

Built by Harland & Wolff, Belfast as a refrigerated cargo vessel. The first in a series which originally was to comprise two ships but later expanded to five and known as the "C" class. Powered by builders' engines which had been adapted to run on "heavy" oil (boiler oil), consuming some 50 tons a day. Although designed for a service speed of 17.5 knots, attained 19.3 knots on trials. 1976 Renamed SEA CONDOR (Panama). 1977 Scrapped at Kaohsiung, Taiwan.
Sister ships: CANOPIC, CARNATIC, CRETIC, CYMRIC.

CYMRIC (1953–1973) Shaw Savill Line

Built by Harland & Wolff, Belfast. July 1954 Fast passage between London and Sydney of 28.5 days. 1973 Transferred to Royal Mail and renamed DURANGO. 1975 Scrapped at Kaohsiung, Taiwan.
Sister ships: CANOPIC, CARNATIC, CEDRIC, CRETIC.

CANOPIC (1954–1975)

Built by Vickers-Armstrongs Ltd., Newcastle. Completed with modification to the refrigerated capacity to cater for the carriage of "chilled" beef instead of frozen beef. Being one of the last of the "C" class to be built, just a hint of streamlining may be observed. 1975 Renamed CAPETAN NICOLAS (Cyprus). 1981 Laid up at Piraeus. 1986 Scrapped in Turkey. Sister ships: CARNATIC, CEDRIC, CRETIC, CYMRIC.

CRETIC (1955–1973)   A. Duncan

Built by Swan Hunter & Wigham Richardson Wallsend. The only one of the "C" class to be powered by Doxford opposed-piston diesels. Reputed to run quieter with this propulsion compared with the other sisters. 1973 Transferred to Royal Mail and renamed DRINA. 1977 Renamed UNITED VIGOUR (Singapore). 1979 Scrapped at Kaohsiung, Taiwan. Sister ships: CANOPIC, CARNATIC, CEDRIC, CYMRIC.

SOUTHERN CROSS (1955–1973)

J.K. Byass

Built by Harland & Wolff Belfast and launched by H.M. Queen Elizabeth. In an attempt to move away from the cargo-passenger schedule, the SOUTHERN CROSS was for passengers only. Proved successful in her round-the-world itinerary. In the mid 1970s it was felt to be too costly to update her structurally and bring her into line with other contemporary cruise liners. 1973 Renamed CALYPSO (Greek) and extensively converted. 1980 Renamed AZURE SEAS (Panama). Sister ship: NORTHERN STAR (122).
(Continued).

SOUTHERN CROSS (1955–1973)   Shaw Savill Line

The absence of cargo space meant that more capacity could be given over to passenger accommodation, hence the machinery space and funnel were placed aft. This photo shows her on Builders trials.

CARNATIC (1957–1973) W. Hubbard

Built by Cammell Laird & Co., Birkenhead, and launched by the wife of the Chairman of Port Line. Completed with holds for the carriage of chilled beef. April 1963 Part of cargo from N.Z. was 10 tons of Totara logs for Maori carvings in N.Z. House, London. 1969–73 Transferred to the Crusader Shipping Co. 1973 Transferred to Royal Mail and renamed DARRO. 1977 Renamed LITSKA K (Cyprus). 1979 Renamed DIMITRA (Panama). 1979 Scrapped in Greece.
Sister ships: CANOPIC, CEDRIC, CRETIC, CYMRIC.

ARABIC (1956–1968)

W. Hubbard

Built by Bremer Vulcan, Vegesack, Germany for carriage of general cargo only. Completed in a record time when order books in British yards were full. 1962 Carried first bulk shipment of tallow from N.Z. 1968 Transferred to Pacific Steam Navigation Company and renamed OROYA. 1970 Renamed PACIFIC RANGER. 1971 Renamed OROYA. 1972 Renamed LAMMA ISLAND (Panama). 1983 Scrapped at Inchon, Korea.
Sister ships: AFRIC, ALARIC, ARAMAIC.

AFRIC (1957–1968) W.S.S. Southampton, Hartwell Bequest

Built by Bremer Vulcan, Vegesack, Germany for carriage of general cargo only. Interiors designed by a young German architect and exterior adopted continental streamlining of superstructure. 1968 Transferred to PSNC and renamed ORITA. 1972 Renamed HONG KONG ISLAND (Panama). 1983 Scrapped at Inchon, Korea.
Sister ships: ALARIC, ARABIC, ARAMAIC.

ARAMAIC (1957–1968)

Real Photographs

Built by Bremer Vulcan, Vegesack, Germany for carriage of general cargo only. Last of the German-built trio, each powered by a single diesel engine. 1968 Transferred to Pacific Steam Navigation Co. and renamed OROPESA. 1970 Renamed PACIFIC EXPORTER. 1970 Renamed OROPESA. 1972 Renamed LANTAO ISLAND (Panama). 1982 Scrapped at Kaohsiung, Taiwan.
Sister ships: AFRIC, ALARIC, ARABIC.

ALARIC (1958–1972)

Built by Harland & Wolff, Glasgow for carriage of general cargo only. Similar in size and appearance to the German-built trio. February 1963 Carried the first export shipment of comb honey from N.Z. to Europe and the U.K. 1972 Renamed IRAN NIRU (Iran). 1977 Renamed RUMI (Iran). 1979 Scrapped in India.
Sister ships: AFRIC, ARABIC, ARAMAIC.

IONIC III (1959–1978)

Built by Cammell Laird & Co., Birkenhead. Known as the "I" Class, a modified version of the earlier "C" class but propelled by a single turbo-charged engine; also operated on heavy oil. Large volume of chilled cargo carried. 1978 Renamed GLENPARVA (Cyprus). 1979 Scrapped at Kaohsiung, Taiwan.
Sister ships: IBERIC, ICENIC, ILLYRIC.

AMALRIC (1960–1977)

Built by Bremer Vulcan, Vegesack, Germany as a refrigerated carrier. 1961 Inaugurated Conference Lines' service between N.Z., West Indies and South American ports. Periodic charters by the Crusader Shipping Company. 1977 Renamed KYMA (Greek). 1985 Renamed MILOS V (Lib). 1986 Scrapped in Pakistan.

A. Duncan

ILLYRIC (1960–1978)

Built by Vickers-Armstrongs (Shipbuilders) Ltd., Newcastle. The first ship in the Company to bear this name. Despite the deceptive appearance of the "I" class, they carried no passengers; the external structure and funnel were streamlined. Nov/ Dec 1963 Slashed time between Newcastle N.S.W. and Sydney. 1978 Renamed CARMILA (Cyprus). 1979 Scrapped at Kaohsiung, Taiwan.
Sister ships: IBERIC, ICENIC, IONIC III.

John Clarkson

ICENIC (1960–1978)

Built by Harland & Wolff, Belfast. Upon her completion the Company had taken delivery of some 250,000 gross tons of shipping since the end of W. W. 2. Total crew 85. 1978 Renamed AEGEAN UNITY (Greek). 1979 Scrapped at Kaohsiung, Taiwan.

Sister ships: IBERIC, ILLYRIC, IONIC III.

IBERIC (1961–1976)   J.K. Byass

Built by Alexander Stephen & Son Ltd., Glasgow. First ship to be built in this yard since the MATAKANA of 1921. The last of the "I" class; the four vessels cost a total of £10 million. Capable of carrying 275 tons of tallow or edible oil in bulk. 1976 Transferred to Royal Mail and renamed DESEADO. 1983 Scrapped at Chittagong, Bangladesh.
Sister ships: ICENIC, ILLYRIC, IONIC III.

NORTHERN STAR (1962–1975)

W. Hubbard

Built by Vickers-Armstrongs (Shipbuilders) Ltd., Newcastle. Launched by H.M. Queen Elizabeth the Queen Mother. 1400 passengers. Improved version of the SOUTHERN CROSS. Experienced h.p. turbine thrust block failure during maiden voyage, delayed schedule by 9 days. 1966 Funnel livery changed and star added to each side. 31 May 1974 The Queen Mother visited the NORTHERN STAR at Southampton. 1975 Scrapped at Kaohsiung, Taiwan.
Sister ship: SOUTHERN CROSS (110).

MEGANTIC (1962–1979)   J.K. Byass

Built by Swan Hunter & Wigham Richardson, Wallsend. Large refrigerated capacity of 581,050 cubic feet and deep tanks for the carriage of tallow or edible oil. First Shaw Savill vessel to be registered at London instead of Southampton. First cargo vessel to bear the new Company livery of grey hull with white riband. 1979 Renamed **DEMETRIOS VENTOURIS/ DIMITRIOS VENTOURIS** (Greek). 1980 Scrapped at Kaohsiung, Taiwan.
Sister ship: MEDIC.

MEDIC (1963–1979)   Swan Hunter & Wigham Richardson

Built by Swan Hunter & Wigham Richardson Ltd., Wallsend. Along with the MEGANTIC was the first cargo vessel built for the Company with full air-conditioning. Also both ships were first built with sewage treatment systems for use in dock basins. The two ships cost £5 million. 1979 Renamed ODYSEFS (Greek). 1987 Scrapped in Pakistan.
Sister ship: MEGANTIC.
(Continued)

MEDIC (1963–1979)   Photo Sami, Port Said

With the reduction of the Shaw Savill fleet in the early 1970s, both the MEDIC and MEGANTIC fulfilled a secondary role as Deck and Engineer cadet training ships.

A. Duncan

ROMANIC (1965–1968)

1944 Built by Harland & Wolff Belfast, as the DRINA for the Royal Mail Line's South American service. 1965 Transferred to Shaw Savill and renamed ROMANIC. 1968 Scrapped Kaohsiung, Taiwan.
Sister ship: RUTHENIC

ZEALANDIC V (1965–1980)   Tom Rayner Collection

Built by Alexander Stephen & Son Ltd., Glasgow. First time Sulzer engines were used in Shaw Savill ships since 1928–built KARAMEA. 1980 Renamed PORT LAUNAY (Greek). 1981 Renamed KHALIJ CRYSTAL (Lib). 1984 Scrapped in Pakistan.
Sister ship: LAURENTIC.

LAURENTIC (1965–1980)

J.K. Byass

Built by Vickers-Armstrongs (Shipbuilders) Ltd., Newcastle. 1980 Renamed SPARTAN REEFER (Greek). 1984 Scrapped in Pakistan.
Sister ship: ZEALANDIC V.

RUTHENIC (1966–1967)
A. Duncan

1944 Built by Harland & Wolff, Belfast as the DURANGO for the Royal Mail Line's South American service. 1966 Transferred to Shaw Savill and renamed RUTHENIC. 1967 Renamed SUSSEX (Greek). 1967 Scrapped at Kaohsiung, Taiwan.
Sister ship: ROMANIC.

J.K. Byass

MAJESTIC (1967–1974)

Built by Alexander Stephen & Son Ltd., Glasgow. The largest refrigerated cargo vessel to be built for Shaw Savill. Reverted to being registered at Southampton. 1974 Renamed N.Z. AORANGI (NZ). 1978 Renamed MYKONOS (Greek). Sister ship: BRITANNIC.

J.K. Byass

BRITANNIC (1967–1974)

Built by Alexander Stephen & Son Ltd., Glasgow. The 31st purpose built vessel since the end of W.W.2 and the last specially ordered for the Company for the meat trade. One of the last six vessels built by Alexander Stephen & Son before it became the Linthouse yard of Upper Clyde Shipbuilders and eventual bankruptcy. 1974 Renamed N.Z. WAITANGI (NZ), 1980 Renamed SERIFOS (Greek).
Sister ship: MAJESTIC.

AKAROA III (1968–1971)   John Clarkson

1959 Built by Harland & Wolff, Belfast as the AMAZON for the Royal Mail Line's South American service. The largest passenger vessel to be completed in the U.K. during 1959 and the first British passenger ship to use A.C. electrical supply throughout. Passenger accommodation for 107 First, 82 Cabin and 275 Third class. 1968 Transferred to Shaw Savill and renamed AKAROA. 479 passengers in one class. 1971 Renamed AKARITA (Norway) converted to a car carrier. 1977 Renamed HUAL AKARITA (Lib). 1980 Renamed AKARITA (Lib). 1982 Scrapped at Kaohsiung, Taiwan. Sister ships: ARANDA, ARAWA IV.

ARAWA IV (1969–1971)

W.S.S. Southampton, Hartwell Bequest

1960 Built by Harland & Wolff, Belfast as the ARLANZA for the Royal Mail Line's South American service. Capacity for 509 passengers in three classes. 1969 Transferred to Shaw Savill and renamed ARAWA. The acquisition of the three Royal Mail liners marked a return to the combined passenger and cargo service. 1971 Renamed HOEGH TRANSIT (Norway), converted to a car carrier. 1972 Renamed HOEGH TROTTER (Norway). 1977 Renamed HUAL TROTTER (Lib). 1980 Renamed TROTTER (Lib). 1981 Scrapped at Kaohsiung, Taiwan.
Sister ships: AKAROA III, ARANDA.

ARANDA (1969–1971)   A. Duncan

1960 Built by Harland & Wolff, Belfast as the ARAGON for the Royal Mail Line's South American service. Capacity for 541 passengers in three classes. 1969 Transferred to Shaw Savill and renamed ARANDA. 1971 Renamed HOEGH TRAVELLER (Norway), converted to a car carrier. 1977 Renamed HUAL TRAVELLER (Lib). 1978 Renamed TRAVELLER (Lib). 1981 Scrapped at Kaohsiung, Taiwan.
Sister ships: AKAROA III, ARAWA IV.

OCEAN MONARCH (1970–1975)

1957 Built by Vickers-Armstrongs (Shipbuilders) Ltd., Newcastle as the **EMPRESS OF ENGLAND** for Canadian Pacific's Liverpool-Canada service. 1970 Purchased by Shaw Savill and renamed **OCEAN MONARCH**. Inaugural cruise to Japan to Expo 70. 1970–71 Refitted by Cammell Laird, Birkenhead at a cost of £1.5 million, to carry 1068 passengers. 1975 Scrapped at Kaohsiung, Taiwan.
Sister ship: **EMPRESS OF BRITAIN**.

ACKNOWLEDGEMENTS

I should like to extend my gratitude and acknowledgement to the following individuals for their support and help without whose assistance this book certainly would not have been written.

Firstly my thanks to Alan S. Mallett for inviting me to contribute this effort towards the Ship Pictorial Publications series. For the illustrations in this book I offer my thanks to those who contributed the majority of the photographs, namely Tom Rayner, Alex Duncan and Keith Byass. From the Shaw Savill Society thanks are due to Graham Pepper and A. C. "Tony", Reed, both former serving officers, who put their respective collections at my disposal.

Other contributors were: Cliff Parsons of the World Ship Photo Library and Paul Kemp of the Imperial War Museum, also Miss Sandra Scott of Lloyds Register.

Finally, thanks to my wife Fiona who typed and corrected the original manuscript.

R.M.S. GOTHIC

BIBLIOGRAPHY

ANDERSON, Roy	*White Star* (T. Stephenson & Sons Ltd. 1964)
BOWEN, Frank	*The Flag of the Southern Cross 1858–1938* (Shaw Savill & Albion, 1939)
CRITCHELL, J. T. & RAYMOND, J.	*A History of the Frozen Meat Trade* (Dawsons of Pall Mall, 1969)
de KERBRECH, Richard P.	*Shaw Savill & Albion, The Post-War Fortunes of a Shipping Empire* (Conway Maritime Press Ltd., 1986)
de KERBRECH, Richard P.	*Harland & Wolff's Empire Food Ships 1934–1948* (Unpublished Manuscript)
GRAHAM, Charles	*Ships of the Seven Seas I* (Ian Allan Ltd. 1947)
HAWS, Duncan	*Merchant Fleets 10–Shaw Savill & Albion* (T.C.L. Publications, 1987)
MABER, John M.	*North Star to Southern Cross* (T. Stephenson & Sons Ltd. 1967)
SHAW SAVILL LINE	*Facts and Figures (1965)*
STEWART, I. G.	*The ships that serve New Zealand Vol I* (A. H. & A. W. Reed, 1964)
WATERS, Sydney, D.	*Shaw Savill Line One Hundred Years of Trading* (Whitcombe & Tombs Ltd., 1961)

INDEX

Notes

1. The notation in Roman Numerals following a ship's name indicates that the ship is the first, second etc vessel of that name in the fleet. No numeral is shown where only one ship bore the name in question. Because the index lists only ships featured in this book there will be certain otherwise inexplicable gaps.

2. Dimensions are Registered Length × Beam × Depth, or, for vessels marked with an asterisk, overall length × beam × load draft.

3. Gross Tonnages are generally those recorded when the ship first entered the Company's service. It should be noted that this figure varies by subsequent modification or change of rules.

4. Engine type is indicated as follows: *Reciprocating:* C = Compound; T = Triple Expansion; Q = Quadruple Expansion followed by the number of cylinders.
   Diesel: D = Oil Engines. 2SC/4SC indicates 2 or 4 stroke cycle. DA/SA indicates Double or Single Acting. *Turbine:* Tur indicates Steam Turbine, preceded by SR (Single Reduction Gearing), or DR (Double Reduction Gearing). *General:* The prefix 2× indicates the number of screws driven by the machinery.

5. Horse Power stated is: (a) For Reciprocating Engines–Indicated
   (b) For Diesel–Brake
   (c) For Turbines–Shaft
   On earlier vessels the power is stated in Nominal Horse Power (NHP). In this case this nomenclature is printed after the figure.

6. The speed given is the service in knots. This could vary according to route and ports of call.

7. No account has been taken of ships that have been substantially modified during their careers, other than 3 vessels which were re-engined.

	Dimensions	Tonnage	Machinery	Power	Speed	Page
AFRIC	*475 × 64.4 × 27.1	6553	1 × D9Cyl 2SCSA	8600	17	114
AKAROA II	550.7 × 67.4 × 44.1	14947	3 × T3Cyl + LP Tur	7500	14.75	59,144
AKAROA III	540 × 78.2 × 28.9	18565	2 × D6Cyl 2SCSA	17000	17.5	132
ALARIC	*473.4 × 64.3 × 27.1	6692	1 × D6Cyl 2SCSA	8500	17	116
AMALRIC	*457.6 × 63.8 × 28.2	7791	1 × D9Cyl 2SCSA	8600	17	118
ARABIC	*475 × 64.4 × 27.1	6553	1 × D9Cyl 2SCSA	8600	17	113
ARAMAIC	*475 × 64.4 × 27.1	6553	1 × D9Cyl 2SCSA	8600	17	115
ARANDA	540 × 78.2 × 28.9	18575	2 × D6Cyl 2SCSA	17000	17.5	134
ARAWA II	460 × 60 × 31	9372	2 × T3Cyl	899 NHP	14	36
ARAWA III	530.9 × 68.3 × 39.9	13837	2 × DR Tur	9000	15	68
ARAWA IV	540 × 78.2 × 28.9	18595	2 × D6Cyl 2SCSA	17000	17.5	133
ATHENIC I	500.25 × 63.25 × 45	12234	2 × Q4Cyl	4400	13	29,30
ATHENIC II	538 × 71.2 × 40.7	15187	2 × SR Tur	14000	17	94
BRITANNIC	546 × 74.8 × 30.1	12228	2 × D8Cyl 2SCSA	15000	19	131
CANOPIC	493.5 × 69.2 × 37.7	11166	2 × D6Cyl 2SCSA	12300	17	108
CARNATIC	493.5 × 69.3 × 37.7	11144	2 × D6Cyl 2SCSA	12300	17	112
CEDRIC	493.5 × 69.3 × 37.7	11232	2 × D6Cyl 2SCSA	12300	17	79,106
CERAMIC I	655.1 × 69.4 × 43.8	18481	3 × T3Cyl + LP.Tur	9000	15	72
CERAMIC II	539.8 × 72.2 × 40.7	15896	2 × DR Tur	17000	17	77,95
COPTIC I	430.2 × 42.2 × 29.4	4367	1 × C2Cyl	2000	13	15
COPTIC II	482.6 × 64.2 × 30.8	8281	2 × D6Cyl 2SCSA	7500	14	56,75
CORINTHIC I	500.25 × 63.25 × 45	12231	2 × Q4Cyl	4400	13	32,73
CORINTHIC II	538 × 71.2 × 40.7	15682	2 × SR Tur	14000	17	93
CRETIC	493.5 × 69.4 × 37.7	11151	2 × D6Cyl 2SCSA	11300	17	109
CRUSADER	210.7 × 35.1 × 21.4	1058	SAILING VESSEL	-	-	12
CYMRIC	493 × 69.2 × 37.1	11182	2 × D6Cyl 2SCSA	12300	17	107
DELPHIC	489.1 × 65.7 × 38.6	10691	2 × D5Cyl 2SCSA	9800	17	100
DOMINION MONARCH	657.6 × 84.8 × 44.5	27155	4 × D5Cyl 2SCSA	32000	19.25	4,76 & 82-90

	Dimensions	Tonnage	Machinery	Power	Speed	Page
DORIC I	440.9 × 44.2 × 29.4	4676	1 × C2Cyl	3280	13	18
			Re-engine T3Cyl			
DORIC II	489.1 × 65.7 × 38.6	10674	2 × D5Cyl 2SCSA	9800	17	99
DUNEDIN I	239.8 × 36 × 20.7	1320	SAILING VESSEL	-	-	11
EMPIRE WAIMANA	See WAIMANA					43
ESPERANCE BAY	See HOBSONS BAY					65
FORDSDALE	500 × 63.2 × 37.4	9949	2 × Q4Cyl	1205 NHP	15	62
GOTHIC I	490.7 × 53.2 × 33.5	7755	2 × T3Cyl	4400	13.5	25,136
GOTHIC II	539.8 × 72.2 × 40.7	15902	2 × DR Tur	17000	17	96,97
HERMINIUS	See WAIMANA					42
HOBSONS BAY	530 × 68 × 43.5	13387	2 × DR Tur	9000	15	65
IBERIC	*510.4 × 70.4 × 31.8	11248	1 × D8Cyl 2SCSA	11300	17	121
ICENIC	*513.25 × 70.4 × 31.8	11239	1 × D8Cyl 2SCSA	11300	17	120
ILLYRIC	*513.25 × 70.4 × 31.8	11256	1 × D8Cyl 2SCSA	11300	17	119
IONIC I	439.9 × 44.2 × 29.4	4748	1 × C2Cyl	3280	13	16,17
			Re-engine Q4Cyl			
IONIC II	500.25 × 63.25 × 45	12232	2 × Q4Cyl	4400	13	31
IONIC III	*512.4 × 70.4 × 30.8	11219	1 × D8Cyl 2SCSA	11300	17	117
JERVIS BAY I	530 × 68 × 43.5	13839	2 × DR Tur	9000	15	66
KARAMEA II	482.6 × 64.2 × 30.8	8281	2 × D6Cyl 2SCSA	7500	14	57
KIA ORA	448.3 × 56.4 × 30.6	6558	2 × T3Cyl	810 NHP	13	35

	Dimensions	Tonnage	Machinery	Power	Speed	Page
KUMARA I	425.7 × 54.1 × 29.8	6034	1 × T3Cyl	678 NHP	12	28
KUMARA II	450.4 × 58.4 × 37.2	7926	2 × T3Cyl	1138 NHP	12	63
LADY JOCELYN	254 × 39 × 24.9	2138	SAILING VESSEL	-	-	14
LARGS BAY	530 × 68 × 43.5	13853	2 × DR Tur	9000	15	67
LAURENTIC	*481.3 × 65.9 × 29.1	7964	1 × D8Cyl 2SCSA	11000	18	128
LINDFIELD I	277.5 × 41.9 × 24.2	2280	SAILING VESSEL	-	-	23
MAHANA	500.9 × 63.3 × 39.6	11796	2 × SR Tur	6000	13	48
MAHIA	477.6 × 63.1 × 39.7	10835	2 × Q4Cyl	5600	13	49
MAIMOA	477.9 × 63 × 31.2	8011	2 × Q4Cyl	1039 NHP	12	52
MAJESTIC	546 × 74.8 × 30.1	12591	2 × D8Cyl 2SCSA	15000	19	130
MAMARI I	360 × 42 × 20.8	3583	1 × T3Cyl	385 NHP	10	21
MAMARI II	455.4 × 56.4 × 30.6	7062	2 × Q4Cyl	808 NHP	13	33
MAMARI III	See ZEALANDIC I					46
MAMILIUS	See ZEALANDIC I					45
MARGARET GALBRAITH	198.5 × 32.2 × 19.9	889	SAILING VESSEL	-	-	13
MATAROA	500.4 × 63.2 × 39.6	12341	2 × DR Tur	6750	15	61
MATATUA II	448 × 56.4 × 30.6	6488	2 × T3Cyl	800 NHP	13	34
MAYFIELD I	277.5 × 41.9 × 24.2	2285	SAILING VESSEL	-	-	24
MEDIC	*537.7 × 71.4 × 32.3	12220	2 × D7Cyl 2SCSA	13600	18	124,125
MEGANTIC	*537.7 × 71.4 × 32.3	12226	2 × D7Cyl 2SCSA	13600	18	123
MORETON BAY	530 × 68 × 43.5	13850	2 × DR Tur	9000	15	64
NEW						78 &
AUSTRALIA	550 × 83.5 × 43.2	20205	4 × Tur. Elec.	18000	18	103-105
NORTHERN STAR	*650 × 83.7 × 26.1	24756	2 × DR Tur	22000	20.5	80,122
OTIRA	450.4 × 58.4 × 37.2	7995	2 × T3Cyl	1138 NHP	12	50
OCEAN MONARCH	600 × 85.2 × 48	25971	2 × DR Tur	30000	21	135

	Dimensions	Tonnage	Machinery	Power	Speed	Page
PAKEHA II	477.5 × 63.1 × 31.3	7899	2 × Q4Cyl	4990	13	39,40
PERSIC	539.8 × 72.2 × 31.9	13594	2 × SR Tur	14000	17	98
RANGATIRA I	356 × 47 × 26.8	4045	1 × T3Cyl	415 NHP	10	22
RANGATIRA II	478 × 61.3 × 31.3	10118	2 × T3Cyl	5600	13	38
RARANGA	477 × 63.2 × 31.3	10040	2 × Q4Cyl	5000	13	47
ROMANIC	*468.8 × 65.3 × 33.3	9785	2 × D6Cyl 2SCDA	1802 NHP	15	126
RUNIC	539.8 × 72.2 × 31.9	13587	2 × SR Tur	14000	17	101
RUTHENIC	*468.8 × 65.3 × 33.3	9801	2 × D6Cyl 2SCDA	1802 NHP	15	129
SUEVIC	539.8 × 72.2 × 31.9	13587	2 × SR Tur	14000	17	102
SOUTHERN CROSS	560 × 78 × 45.3	20204	2 × DR Tur	20000	20	110,111
TAINUI I	439.6 × 46.3 × 28.9	5031	1 × T4Cyl	?	13	19,20
TAINUI II	477.8 × 61.1 × 31	9957	2 × T3Cyl	1086 NHP	14	37
TAIROA	478 × 63 × 31.2	7983	2 × Q4Cyl	1039 NHP	12	51
TAMAROA	500.4 × 63.2 × 39.6	12405	2 × DR Tur	6750	15	60,74
TARANAKI	482.6 × 64.2 × 30.8	8286	2 × D6Cyl 2SCSA	7500	14	54,55
THEMISTOCLES	500.6 × 62.3 × 39.4	11231	2 × Q4Cyl	6000	14	58
TOKOMARU	425 × 58.2 × 23.6	6238	1 × T3Cyl	521 NHP	11	26
WAIMANA	477.6 × 63.1 × 31.1	10389	2 × T3Cyl	5600	13	41
WAIMARAMA	516.9 × 70.4 × 31.3	11092	2 × D6Cyl 2SCDA	13200	16	81
WAIPAWA	516.2 × 70.4 × 32.4	10784	2 × D10Cyl 4SCSA	9500	16	70
WAIRANGI I	516.2 × 70.4 × 32.4	10779	2 × D10Cyl 4SCSA	9500	16	71
WAIRANGI II	521.4 × 70.4 × 40.5	13478	2 × D6Cyl 2SCDA	10000	16	92
WAIWERA I	425.7 × 54.1 × 29.8	6237	1 × T3Cyl	678 NHP	12	27
WAIWERA II	516.2 × 70.4 × 32.4	10782	2 × D10Cyl 4SCSA	9500	16	69
WAIWERA III	521.4 × 70.4 × 40.5	12028	2 × D6Cyl 2SCDA	10000	16	91

	Dimensions	Tonnage	Machinery	Power	Speed	Page
ZEALANDIA	215.6 × 35.1 × 20.3	1165	SAILING VESSEL	-	-	10
ZEALANDIC I	477.5 × 63.1 × 31.5	10898	2 × Q4Cyl	596 NHP	14	44
ZEALANDIC II	482.6 × 64.2 × 30.8	8281	2 × D6Cyl 2SCSA	7500	14	53
ZEALANDIC V	*481.3 × 65.9 × 29.1	7946	1 × D8Cyl 2SCSA	11000	18	127

FAREWELL

Alan Mallett Collection

After 40 years' good service between The United Kingdom and New Zealand, AKAROA was sold to Belgian shipbreakers in May 1954.